Long Distance

Long Distance

~

Poems

Mark Vinz

MWPH Books
Fairwater, Wisconsin

Acknowledgements

Some of the poems in this collection have been previously published in the following, sometimes in slightly different form:

Periodicals

Ascent, Flyway, Great Midwestern Quarterly, Great River Review, High Plains Literary Review, Lake Region Review, Midwest Quarterly, North Coast Review, North Dakota Quarterly, Ruah, Saturday's Poem at the Middlewesterner, Sidewalks, Solo, South Dakota Review, Third Coast.

"Midway," "The Boy in the Woods," "Intro to Children's Lit," and "Finding My Way" first appeared in *The Hudson Review*.

Anthologies

After the Storm: Poems on the Persian Gulf War; Getting By: Stories of Working Lives; Minnesota Poetry Calendar, The Next Parish Over: A Collection of Irish-American Writing; Pocket Poems; Seeing the Blue Between: Advice and Inspiration for Young Poets; Visiting Emily: Poems Inspired by the Life and Work of Emily Dickinson; Visiting Frost: Poems Inspired by the Life and Work of Robert Frost; Wherever Home Begins: 100 Contemporary Poems

Cover photo: "Red River Valley" by Mark Vinz

Special thanks to Jay Meek for his editorial suggestions for early versions of the manuscript, and to Joe Richardson, who helped in so many ways.

MWPH Books
PO Box 8, Fairwater, WI 53931
ISBN: 0-9746499-2-9

for Betsy, of course

Backroads

Life & Times

Tour Guide

Mementos

Backroads

Directions

All around me storm clouds sweep the prairie,
each road a thin ribbon laid between
the hills and herds of grazing cows,
with sudden winds that rock the car
through every dip and curve. 40 miles
to the interstate, and not a town in sight.

My father couldn't understand the
trouble I had with directions. Every time
I'm lost I think of him, the country sense
I never had—the way he always knew
just where we were, the quickest routes,
the name of every crop in those mysterious
fields, and where to find the best cafés.

40 miles to the interstate, the heavy smell
of new cut hay, and somewhere in those
darkening hills and rain, lights are coming on,
the ones I still can't see but know are there.

Red River Valley

From time to time, there comes a need to
drive the backroads, past meandering streams
we didn't expect, the tiny graveyards
and falling-down sheds, the lone trees
plowed around so carefully.
In a place this flat and endless,
each small variation seizes the eye.

The car tracks eastward to the gradual rise
of glacial beaches. Beyond are hills
with woods and lakes, but we turn north
along the valley's edge, a broad horizon
cradling clouds, and then to the west,
past land that holds a dozen different
kinds of hay bales. Not far from home
by country reckoning we stop beside
a field edged with a swath of zinnias—
a quarter mile of blossoms, bright-headed
in waning light. It's getting late, but
still we watch the flowers—what we
won't forget those last dark miles
where other lights come out to meet us.

Flat Country

after Dana Gioia

Give me a landscape where the sky is huge
with scudding, booming clouds—no walls of trees
obscuring hovering hawks, except along
the riverbanks where cottonwood and willow
watch meandering currents, ox-bowed in
their own stubborn time.
                              This is a place where
fences seem an afterthought, no mountains
to distract the eye from bluestem haze and
spikes of blazing star—spirit's reckoning
that rises with each plume of dust or smoke.

Perspective is the ground that creeps up from
the valley floor, reminding us of what
is coming from a long way off—rippling
the prairie grass, another universe
that spreads out all around us, at our feet.

The Lay of the Land

Heavy-headed grass grows tall beside the
gravel road, looking like a narrow wheat field,
a half-mile against the edge of the forest.
My neighbor frees some kernels in his palms—
see, he says, that bluish cast means rye,
not wheat, as if I should have known, as if
anybody should have known. They're like that
out here in the woods, proud of what they've learned,
what they've built—from roads to cabins. Most days
I hear the whine and roar of their machines.
Most evenings they survey the lakeshore from
immense pontoon boats, craning necks to see
who's home—another kind of expertise.

Chilly winds and rain this week, and scarcely
a boat on the water. For hours I've watched
the waves and leaves and listened for the loons.
It's something to do when your work is words,
when you're never sure of where you're going.

For the Season

Blue Cloud Abbey, South Dakota

As we drove up from the valley,
giant hay bales lay scattered like
pieces from some child's game
abandoned hopelessly. Clouds
moved in at dusk, thick along the
snow-patched slopes. This world
seems angrier tonight than usual,
as icy winds flap window blinds,
but then a distant organ sounds as
voices rise in prayer, reminding us
we're safe and warm and far from
all the old routines we've left behind.
Time renews itself again, and now
we think of those we care about,
and walk outside as tower bells
break over us in waves, and watch—
far beyond those clouds we can't see
in the dark, the first star, flickering.

Lines

for Joe

Out in the boat last night we watched still air
suddenly filling with mayflies—as far
as we could see or move they came in waves.
Today their delicate remains are lined
on cabin screens, and once again the air
is thick with wings, this time from dragonflies,
dark and deliberate in their searching.

A single day, the mayflies come and go,
and now we see their helpless tracks laid down
on top of water where fish keep rising.
Only by chance we notice how these lives
complete themselves—another set of lines
to read and ponder for their grace alone,
another quickly disappearing page.

Reply

"For all the history of grief
An empty doorway and a maple leaf."
      —Archibald MacLeish, from "Ars Poetica"

Perhaps I never understood those lines
and maybe never will.
An empty doorway: what once was there
and now is lost to all but memory.
A maple leaf: I turn the image
in my head and start with green,
though it's never green for long.

Today we drove two hundred miles
to look at leaves. It's what we do
each fall, wherever we are—
what the children joke about,
this need for leaf-watching.
But not just any leaves: the maple
soars in red, from earth to fire to blood,
and in the day's last slant of sun
a kind of respite, more than grief,
that we too might return in a new season.
Now, as winds rasp through the trees,
I have to say good night again
to this empty doorway, this stubborn page,
another leaf—turned, unturned, and turning—
in all this dark, a spot of glowing red.

Glimpses

for Thom

They'd warned us of deer on the roads—
that something was making them restless,
that we'd never see them in time. Take it
easy, they said, if you want to get home—
but there at the edge of the deepest woods,
the highway was slick with blood
and parts—hindquarters in the ditch,
the glimpse of antlers, something to
make them restless, those big semis
speeding toward cities and daylight.
We wondered aloud what the drivers
could have seen, our own car shrinking
to wheels and eyes, trying to take it easy
on that crowded road—where the only thing
to leap out startled from the dark was us.

Prairie Storm

Driving back late from Winnipeg
we watch the border sky turn nightmare red.
All around us patches of fire and smoke
with scattered figures moving on the prairie.
A simple explanation, the customs agent says:
when the crops are in, the fields are burned.

To keep awake we listen to songs on the radio—
lost love and heartache, with bulletins of
world-wide storms, a threat of war continuing.
Easy enough to understand, isn't it?
After a harvest, what's left must burn.
All the long drive home we watch the sky for fire.

Guide to the Northwoods

The really big fish, he tells us,
are the money sport around here.
You don't know what fanatics are
till you've met those muskie fishermen,
the ones who'll do anything to get a lunker—
like kittens, he says. You can't find kittens
around here in the summer—those guys
put ads in the papers, go door to door
and ask for them—black and white ones
are the best, they say. Imagine it,
casting out a kitten in a harness rig.
When they hit that water, they really
flail and claw, and then, if you're lucky,
all those big teeth rising from beneath
like some kind of crocodile. He holds
his hands to mimic jaws, then stops
abruptly. Of course, I've never used
kittens myself—don't get me wrong!
And then he smiles a little too shyly.
Come on, he says, I know a place
we'll get some good fish, even if
we're in the doldrums now—you know,
you should have come last week, before
the lake turned over, but don't worry,
we're going to find you your limit.

Dragging Broadway

Weekends they line up for the parade,
in from every town for miles—
six blocks up and six blocks back,
while the city debates what to do about it.
The noise, the traffic, the threat of beer
and worse, much worse, they say.
You know kids, that trick of being seen
and heard.
                    The tired cop keeps watching
from his motorbike—in every passing window
another face he knows. What's there to do,
anyway? Every week the circle dance grows
longer, each car braying different songs.
The words keep changing, too, the words
keep moving like a pulse, but every
now and then an old familiar tune—
until there's nothing left again but
empty streets and small lights burning
in the safe and songless dark.

Work, for the Night is Coming

Old man across the street,
retired early with one good arm,
waits patiently till 8 o'clock
to mow his close-cropped grass
and wash his already-shining car,
to re-edge the walk and prune
whatever branch seems wayward.
He'll paint the house again this year,
repatch each crack, replant each shrub.

The children seldom visit anymore,
he doesn't talk to neighbors, and
his wife still works—he drives her
there and picks her up, and now
it's nearly noon. All sidewalks have
been scrubbed kitchen-table clean,
the hose re-coiled, hung carefully
in the garage, where each tool
rests in its most proper place.

Old man across the street,
who's not as old as he might look,
surveys the garden that he weeded
yesterday, birds lined up on wires,
a neighbor with a speedboat on a trailer,
chattering children streaming by on bikes.
And now, another afternoon spreads out
so fiercely bright beyond the blinds
he draws in every room, one by one by one.

Center Café

Well, you're in town, then. The boys
from the class reunion wander in
and take their places in the corner booth,
just as they might have fifty years ago—
grayer, balder, wearing hats announcing
places far away. Their conversation
rises, falls to the inevitable—a missing
friend who worked right up until the end,
another who is long past traveling. Smiles
grow distant as their silence overtakes
the room. The busy waitress pauses,
nods. She's always known the boys.

Nguyet Café

For CWT

It doesn't matter we're uncertain
how to pronounce the names—
the food is what we've come for,
the service quiet and intent.
It doesn't matter that the place is dingy
and the bathroom door won't close—
back in the cluttered kitchen where
the lone woman smiles and disappears
behind a veil of unfamiliar smells.
It doesn't even matter that a
stuffed walleyed pike swims
on the wall above us—token of the
strange new land that for a moment
holds us here, guests and hosts alike,
the men in white shirts perched at
a table with lilting cadences of
word and hand, the children
in the corner gathered by a TV set,
wearing T-shirts bright with messages
their fathers must wonder about.
Tell your friends, the owner says
with bobbing smiles, beside his new
cash register —to which is taped a
snapshot of a family under palms
and a hand-printed card announcing
chopsticks are available upon request.

P.O.W.

Elwood laughs alone tonight,
bellows something indecipherable.
It's funny how they always sound the
same, old men toothless in dingy bars.
Elwood squints and curses at another
empty can of Pabst. What year was it
when the Chinese swept across the Yalu
like some kind of nightmare tide?
Mother died in '56, Father '54.
Don't you remember when it was
those Air Force sons of bitches lost the war?

Elwood mutters, flaps his empty cheeks
at us, then lurches up and down the bar
in search of faces that remember howitzers.
Your fly is open, someone says but
Elwood doesn't give a damn for fly boys.
He scrubs two fingers through his ragged crewcut,
sits back down and shrugs and fumbles for
his Pall Malls in his shirt. Where were we?
Elwood says to empty beer can rows like
spent artillery shells. Where were we
when those sons of bitches gave away the farm?

Breakdown

I'm not afraid to buy American,
the tow truck man says.
Behind us, my old car bounces
from the potholes on U.S. 75,
but there's no need to look back.
It's probably thrown a rod—one of
those terms I've heard before
but never had to believe.
The tow truck man talks on—
of moving to the small town
from the city, of why cold
winters don't bother him
and foreigners do, of how
with Triple-A this ride is
cheaper than a cab would be.
40 miles to home in fading light—
it could be worse. I didn't
drive the back roads after all,
managed to coast and clatter
to the station at the edge of town—
where they simply shook their heads.
Sometimes this rig is like a hearse,
the tow truck man says, but
it could be worse. Just look at those
snow clouds moving in, but so what?
Nothing new to us. Happy to be here,
no matter what it costs.

Russian Olives

Along the highways you can find them
abandoned to whatever will survive.
Known as weeds by some, they
thrive into scatterings of small trees—
what once was brought by settlers for
their hedges and windrows, now wild,
unruly as a pack of stray dogs,
their silvery coats flaring out
from all the surrounding green.
How quickly they grow, as if
we didn't see them only yesterday, or
simply didn't look—among the wagon ruts
forever tracking westward from the cities.

Lilacs

When they came West, the women brought them—
gifts, perhaps, from mothers to daughters
they knew they'd never see again—
for beauty's sake, a piece of home
to plant beside the house or ring a yard,
a shady place to nurture children.

Around the countryside you still
can find them growing wild in clumps
where long ago the farmsteads stood,
reminders of what's lost or hidden—
those final, necessary boundaries
of all that couldn't be cut down.

Great Plains

I delight in the things I discover
right within reach. —Ted Kooser

Try to think of one more imagination game
to keep you going, maybe what a long, dull
road trip might be compared to—like a job
you hate but need to keep to stay alive.
Or remember the dream you wake from in panic,
the one that won't let go of you for days,
its own tedious roads that keep you looping
back upon yourself. You sing along
with some melody beneath the static.

Try to remember loneliness is supposedly
the beholder's making, even as the sun
slips into heavy clouds it will not
rise from, the dark fields growing into night,
until you notice lights in the distance—
soon startled by bright beams coming at you,
the giant combines churning, the grain trucks
lining up in sheets of billowing dust.

Try to get it down, all of it—the world
within a world you couldn't imagine
till right now—so that when you wake,
finally, you can still feel that dust
beneath your eyelids, the prairie earth
you'll need to pare from fingernails, the
disappearing road still rising up to meet you.

Life & Times

The Room You Go Back to

*"It is all around you and inside you, and for reasons
you cannot know, it contains everything up you did or
felt or thought."*
— B.H. Fairchild, from "The Memory Place"

It was the kitchen, or a succession
of them—the places tend to disappear,
but a yellow formica table always remains,
my father sitting there in his undershirt,
reading the evening paper, sipping
beer from a glass, and my mother
standing at the sink, washing something—
dishes or vegetables or jars for canning—
hair pressed damp against her neck
and forehead, while my little sister
squirms in her highchair or playpen,
thwacking a wooden spoon. And here
I come in my rolled-up jeans and
cowboy hat, holding a shot glass for
my ounce of Shell's or Stag or Grain Belt—
whatever beer has been on sale—which
tickles my nose and leaves an aftertaste,
while the years outside the windows
flicker by like those Burma Shave signs
on the roads my father has to travel
three weeks out of four. But for now
he turns on the red plastic radio to
what he calls a Twi-Night Doubleheader
and says again someday he'll have to
get time off and take me to a game.

But that will be a long while yet,
another kitchen, another city, another
twilit afternoon, as something frying
on the stove makes our mouths water,
and my mother smiles at her boys,
as she calls us, silent at the table
with their beer and ballgames, waiting for
the crack of a bat, the streak of light
rising against the lengthening shadows.

A Green Hill, Far Away

It was the place the wrinkled people lived,
a small log cabin on the highest hill.
What I remember best is silent days
of never-ending work—goats to be milked
and gardens to be tended. They never
gave me much to do, only warned about
the neighbor's cows, that menacing horde
just beyond the barbed-wire fence, ready to
trample any wandering boy. When I dared
to drink the warm goat's milk, they had to smile,
then left me free to roam green boundaries
alone, until the time for rides to town
with cans of fresh milk in an old black car,
motor shut off on the long downgrades
and big trucks coming up behind us, blasting
their air horns. I shrink down into the seat,
trying hard to get my bearings again,
but all those steep green hills look just the same,
the herds of silent, staring goats and cows.

Dodge Ball

There must have been a dozen
different ways to play it.
Teachers had their own ideas,
of course—like how the girls
should be involved. It was
always worse with girls, who
somehow had to be impressed.
With boys it was simple power,
one more opportunity to teach
the fat and weak their place.

Now that I remember, there was
always something new to learn—
like the version called Squeeze,
with a lone dodger in the middle
as the circle slowly shrinks.
Throw it faster, we all shout,
knowing that any hit counts.
Throw it harder, we all shout—
hits that hurt are the ones that last.

Bad Seed

When my parents made me go to Sunday school
they'd always ask when I got home
just what I'd learned. Nothing, I'd say—
they told some stupid stories, like that one
about farming. Some of the kids pretended
it was a big deal, but what did we really care about
crops, anyway, the good seed springing forth to
golden wheat for harvest while the weeds got burned?
Or how about those baskets of bread and fish
the teacher cut out in felt, chirping away about
mountains and multitudes, as if she'd want to eat
that stuff for supper?
                              No, what I really learned was
that I hated sermons even if they fed you afterwards,
that there were people I wanted to hit because they'd
go along with anything, that someday I'd be brave enough
to keep on walking past those huge church doors,
all the way to my favorite place—the vacant lot
where there was no wheat, where the only thing
springing forth was weeds and grasshoppers—
flat and clear and familiar in the burning light.

Art Education

When it came to drawing, I couldn't find a way
to make the lines and colors come out right
and hated those who could—girls, mostly.
I grew up expecting girls to be impossibly
good at anything beyond sports.
Then one day in 4th grade I took my crayons
and copied a picture from one of my books—
a cowboy on a charging horse, twirling a
lasso above his head. The teacher tacked it
to the bulletin board, and some of those
girls who'd never even spoken to me
had to admit it was really good.

Then I wondered if they'd ever see the book
I copied from—my own poor horses looked like
dogs or cows, and I hadn't tried people since
someone laughed at my 1st grade smears.
If they ever found out, they never let on,
and now I still can see it in my head—
my cowboy so resolved and strong,
the lines and colors coming out just right
for one amazing moment—before that other,
more familiar self stepped in and tore it up—
and never said a word until he had to.

Learning the Ropes

Fourth grade was the first real test,
that old woman who scared us into stones
every time she looked up from her desk.
But nothing could top those tales of
the fifth grade teacher in the room
next door—older, meaner, bigger,
she was the one who'd really get us.
We only had to hear the thumping
on the coat room wall to know
that she was in there banging heads,
hanging kids on hooks like slabs of beef.
Those horror stories grew, as we did,
ruled by everything we didn't know.

My family moved away that summer, so I
never did find out what that thumping was—
but on the last day of school, when we
learned that Old Miss Fifth Grade
had recently decided to retire, the
strangest thing was the disappointment
we all felt. No one could begin to explain it,
milling around those suddenly empty rooms,
murmuring our helpless goodbyes.

Original Sin

It would go on my permanent record,
the teacher said, marked in ink that wouldn't
come off, not ever—in some huge old
dusty book, I guessed, whose pages would
always follow me. What else was in it,
from how far back? I'd wake some mornings
imagining that. The strangest thing was
how soon I could forget just what it was
I'd done—only that teacher's frowning glare,
while just behind her on the classroom wall
George Washington looked down. He never lied,
and how I hated him for that, hated
every shining example they gave me,
to which I knew I'd never measure up—
standing there trembling beside my desk,
wondering again what she was writing down.

Surviving Grandma's House

After I'd sewn a thread right through my finger
I kept away from that old treadle-run machine,
trying to amuse myself, as the grownups put it,
with something that didn't make much noise—
certainly not the songs I could plink out on the piano.
I hadn't learned how to read books yet,
or maybe it was summer laziness.
The dead fox stole that hung in the closet,
the painted cast-iron terrier in the hall—
we all seemed prisoners of some other time.
At least I had the cards in Grandpa's desk
to invent new ways to play solitaire
whenever I got tired of the old ones,
or that big jar of stray and mismatched buttons
I could spread into opposing armies
and shoot across the floor like tiddly-winks.
I wonder if somehow I knew even then
this was a place I'd keep coming back to,
even when there was nothing left of it
except what mysteriously got saved—
a few stray buttons and agate marbles,
a pair of chopsticks, three watch fobs, and
rings of keys that don't open anything.

Bathtub Existentialist

Baths always meant it was time to come in
and get ready for bed, a good time to start
thinking about tomorrow, my mother said—
which I usually didn't want to think about—
a good time to examine myself and dream of
another body—the one that wouldn't betray me.

Grownups never seemed to take so many baths,
especially not my grandmother, who warned
they weakened you—I had to love her for that,
especially those nights I got sent back
to scour that telltale ring with Ajax,
one more of those things I couldn't get right.

Alone in the bathroom, washcloth in my
pasty, wrinkled fingers, I'd scrub it all away,
scrub myself till there was nothing left.
They'd be sorry, when they searched for me—
the brilliant boy who used to live here,
that ultimate gurgle, swirling down the drain.

Intro to Children's Lit

Alice's strange world had nothing on mine—
the Queen of Hearts a maiden aunt who drank,
Mad Hatter parties every day at school,
what must have been an evil sorcerer
who conjured clouds of fire and ash at church,
and even a wicked witch—the granny
who could blink me into a frog at will.

I kept hoping I'd be a prince one day
but somehow knew I'd never make it up
Rapunzel's golden hair, or even find it.
Lost in the woods I prayed for magic spells,
a fairy godmother, or luck like Jack's,
for in my beanstalk dreams, something immense
was smelling my blood, gaining ground each night.

Market Share

In 7th grade, when math was still general,
and just before those tangled roads of algebra
would lose and leave me, our teacher decided
we should learn something about the stock market.
Each of us would get a thousand dollars to spend
on imaginary stocks, then watch the prices
for a month, with a prize for the biggest gain.

I'd never heard the term Blue Chips, but that's what
I chose—Standard Oil, General Motors, Westinghouse,
names that sounded so substantial—and raced home
each afternoon to wait for the newspaper.
Delirious with every rise, I made a hundred bucks,
the best of anyone I talked to—until the day
we figured our final gains and losses,
and this crazy kid in the back row tripled his stake
on wildcat drilling and silver mines.
Some of his stocks had even split and multiplied,
mysteriously as loaves and fishes. Our teacher
tried to explain, but I had a hard time listening,
career dreams trampled in one bullish stampede.
Safe and sorry, I wasn't even number two,
and our next math lesson looked harder yet—
balancing a checkbook, with more of that money
I somehow knew I wasn't ever going to get.

Eighth Grade

Our biology teacher should have known better
if anybody should. "When I call on you," she said,
"You'll stand beside your desks when you recite."
She had to know those helpless and amazing things
that kept happening in our pants, the way we boys
would slide from our desks half-crouched
and spit out any answer, then slip back—
she, with her mustache and stark gray suits.

English was another matter, that sweet new teacher
who thought she could control us by ringing a little bell,
which tinkled constantly beneath our raucous joy.
More than once, we made her cry—
we, who couldn't seem to help ourselves.

Years later, someone said those first months
in the classroom turned out to be her last,
and now I still can see her standing there in bright,
tight-fitting floral prints, so shy and beautiful and alone.
How could she know that with biology next hour
we simply had to give her everything she never deserved?
How could we know what we met in those two rooms
were the women who'd define us all our lives?

About the Size of It

You want me to buy clothes to fit
your head, not the rest of you,
my father always said, but *he* was
the one who came home with
whatever was on sale. I can't
remember growing up with many
pairs of socks or pants or underwear
not marked *irregular*. With shoes
it was even worse—whatever
mocked me the most by lasting.
Shirts were supplied by grandmothers
who sewed, one of whom got material free
from the local feed mill. Good cotton
cloth, my father said, but *he* never had
to wear those florid prints to school.
My other grandmother worked in nylon—
old man shirts you could see through.
Good for you in the heat, she said.

There were exceptions, of course—
the aunt who bought me cowboy boots
that pinched my toes, the time in junior high
I sneaked off and bought my own shirts,
the ones that shrank and bled.
Even now I can't find much that fits right.
Rump-sprung and frayed, my wardrobe
drives my wife to catalogues for presents—
even if they're not on sale,
even if she knows that most of them
will be returned, and even if she's
come to understand I can't help hear
my father chuckling at his spendthrift son,
the one with the well-dressed head.

Midway

It took a long time to buy that first ticket,
even with the dares of those few summer friends
I'd always find at the county fair. We'd ride
the Tilt-O-Whirl until we reeled and puked
whatever forbidden food we'd been eating,
but the Tilt-O-Whirl was safely earth-bound,
not like the rickety ferris wheel, where I'd watch
amazed—that noisy belt, those greasy gears,
and high above, the small seats teetering.
It had to be ridden, I didn't know why—
with an older boy who said it would be fine,
who laughed all the way up as I clung to the bar
giddy with fear I'd never felt—until our seat crested
the top, and I knew I'd be back, again and again,
directionless above the blur of lights that stretched
to summer's end, and all those huge gears turning.

Worlds

*"No women were my heroes...
Not in the 50's."* —Paul Janeczko

Women weren't my heroes either—
they simply raised me.
Grandmothers, aunts, teachers,
and of course, my mother—
bristling with rules but always there
to send me off to that world
where boys were busy being boys.
Men were somewhere farther off—
father, uncles, preacher in the pulpit
raining down the law. Theirs
was a world of glimpses, like
those pictures taped to my walls—
cowboys riding off to impossible endings,
ballplayers I could never hope to be.
What I knew best was this:
friends were everything, in backyards
or in basement rooms, exchanging
our confusion like a sacred text.
Someday we'd be men,
though we weren't sure how,
and our heroes were only
what we longed for—not women,
not yet, their ways impossible,
their vast world bounded
by what we couldn't see or touch,
by all those necessary things
we didn't want to know.

The Hard Way

After school there'd usually be a fight.
We seldom knew why, or even cared—
caught in the circle of shouts and eyes
that thickened around two bodies
clenched and rolling on the playground.
Except for split lips and shiners,
no one really got hurt. Most days
they'd simply walk away, arms draped
around each other as if they'd learned
something—until the next time
it got started, the rest of us left to wonder
when it would be our turn. Once or twice
it was even two girls who fought,
but there were grownups too—the ones
who had to let us know who was in charge.
I still remember one poor kid, slapped silly
by the shop teacher we heard had been a
wrestler, the one they said was ambushed by
somebody's father with a tire iron. But that
was only rumor. Heads down, mouths shut,
we studied facts: This was junior high, and
in spite of everything, one day we'd graduate—
to another place we didn't want to imagine.

Seasons

We only went to ballgames when the Yankees
came to town, my father's team since childhood.
He'd talk about Berra or Rizzuto
like they were family members, while I rooted for
the Dodgers—Hodges, Reese and Robinson—
and got used to losing each World Series bet.
Next year, he'd say, and smile—but I could
hear the creaking wheels of doom already.

It wasn't long before the Bums left Brooklyn
and we were moving too, to Kansas City—
a wrong-league town, but one that had a team.
I tried to like the A's, already hopeless
by the end of April, and then one night
I watched Mantle hit one out from both sides
of the plate, and for that moment, the past
was gone—my father and I cheered together.

But everything else was disappearing too—
it would be a long time till the next game
with my father. I had packed away my
baseball gear and found a summer job
so I could have a car and follow dreams
perhaps impossible as winning seasons.
The one thing I knew would never change was
my father, and that smile I'd never forget.

Child Labor

My first job was at a golf course
selling soda, snacks, and beer
in a shack beside the 10th tee.
I was 15, lost in dreams of cars and girls
but wondering more than anything
if I'd ever own a set of clubs and
someday get to play that course myself.

I never did, but learned a few things
anyway, like how to smoke and swear
and sample every kind of candy bar
and chips, and then the beer—
six brands or eight, who can remember
when they all tasted the same?

What I do recall is that each hour
I made 50 cents plus all the tips
I never saw. There I'd wait
in the rising heat of afternoon,
sipping Coors or Budweiser, trying to
figure out a way to get a clubhouse job,
keeping my eye on every small
white ball until it disappeared into
the green and shimmering distance.

Music Education

For David and Bill

The first time, it was Louis Armstrong
at the Kansas City auto show, where
my father took me to see the new cars—
which I mainly ignored, perched on
some shiny bumper not 20 feet from
the bell of that magnificent horn and
something so grand, even then I knew
I'd never be the same. I was 15,
and not long after that it was Basie,
then Ellington, with their big bands rocking
the shopping center parking lot not far
from where we lived. Hard to believe that
right here were those names from records
I 'd been listening to, and soon enough
there'd be Bird and Monk and Benny Goodman
hour after hour in my room, Miles at the
Blackhawk, Brubeck and Barnett, and even
Irving Fazola, whose *Clarinet Marmalade*
I'd nearly worn right off the vinyl.
And then one day most of the records stopped.
I could blame rock and roll, or cars and beer
and all those girls we kept searching for,
or maybe the way life faded into summers
working at the flour mill with a loading crew
of down-on-their-luck musicians waiting
to be side men for whatever band might
happen through town. But there weren't many,
and it wouldn't be long till that wide-eyed boy
was heading off to college, the road
that leads farther and farther from home.
But there'd always be the music, somewhere,
the first poetry he ever knew and loved.

Beast of Burden

Summers meant the flour mills and
good money as a sampler for the USDA,
an endless circle from packing floor
to boxcars, where I had to check the bags.
The loading crews all knew I was a
college boy, told me every day
I'd better stay in school or I'd end up
like them—some dumb animal doomed
to carry hundred-pounders on his back.
When they asked me what I was studying,
I'd lie and tell them chemistry. They'd
smile at that, knowing the white coats
in the lab had decent jobs, and out of
the heat, too—120 degrees most days
on those sidings. Sometimes I'd help
carry a few bags from the chute, learning
to flip them into neatly forming tiers.
Just when I'd feel good about my muscles,
they'd say again I'd better stay in school or
they'd kick my ass all the way to St. Louis.
There we'd stand in those stifling boxcars,
sharing a forbidden smoke whenever
the conveyor belt broke down, talking
about the icy beers we'd be having soon—
when they'd go their way and I'd go mine,
covered with flour dust and sweat
that dried into paste across our skin
and took a long time to scrub off.

Minimum Wage

Most Saturdays I worked the night shift
at the Kansas City *Star*—what they called
the slave labor crew, assembling the
Sunday editions—winos, drifters, dropouts,
a few high school kids and guys home
from college looking for a little extra cash.
If we got lucky we'd be done by 5 a.m.,
drag our aching muscles home and swear
this would be the last time, though we also
knew we'd probably be back—the place
they'd hire you, no questions asked.

The mail room regulars were big shots
on Saturdays, every one of them a foreman
screaming orders, making sure none of us
was hiding in the john or sleeping behind
a stack of papers. Once I asked the loudest
if he'd ever heard of Hemingway. Sure,
he said—I fired that greaser months ago.
So watch it, or I'll be firing your ass too.

One time I had to get a paycheck
on a weekday morning and discovered
all those foremen did exactly what
the rest of us did on the weekends.
None of them would acknowledge me—
or maybe they never noticed, heads down,
skin turned gray from years of printer's ink,
hacking from the paper dust that filled the air.
That was the week I never came back.

Job Description

Three nights a week I tended bar
at a college joint where all
we could serve was 3.2 beer,
mastering the lingo as I went along:
two of anything, *a pair*, and three,
a crowd; *Rocky in the Armor*,
a can of Coors, and 86, *kill the order*.
Most of it slips, but I do remember
girls who weren't impressed by
bartenders, there were no tips,
and a big part of the job was
pouring drinks for the owner,
a local legend who kept his whiskey
in a paper bag beneath the bar.
When he couldn't stand up I'd have
to drive him home, hurrying back
for a few free rounds, to blast
the jukebox and help the waiters
sweep the place up. The only rule
was *never turn the lights up high*.
We all were learning, even then,
what we couldn't bear to see.

Foreign Exchange

Benny Martinelli used to tell stories
about the North End. When I gave
him a ride home after work one day
we had to tour his neighborhood—
every house where a relative lived,
which was every house for blocks.
His mother said I looked like a
good boy, but his father only
wanted to know where I came from.
When I mentioned going away to
college in the fall, all conversation
stopped. What the hell did he know
anyway? his father said. Just a
lousy cobbler, but he had friends.

Benny told me later not to worry
about it—things had been hard for
his family. Next time, he'd come
to my house out in the suburbs,
bring his camera and take some
shots of the places my people lived.
I had to tell him there weren't any,
and then it seemed time for me to go.
His mother waved from the steps,
his father stayed inside, and Benny
snapped a picture as I drove away,
shouting for me to smile, that he'd
send me a copy if anything turned out.

The Boy in the Woods

He lived behind us half a mile through trees
and wanted to be my friend—to teach me
how to recognize each kind of bark or leaf,
out stalking rabbits with bow and arrow.
Then he showed me his pellet gun,
the one time he took me back to his house,
run-down and gray among leafless branches.
The only color I remember was from
a pile of wings. I had to look them up
in my father's bird book at home—
oriole and tanager, bluejay, cardinal,
goldfinch, mourning dove—and then
I packed away my hunting gear for good.

After that, I saw him only once, at a game,
sitting by himself in a corner of the stands,
sighting an imaginary barrel at the players.
Someone said he quit school when he turned
sixteen—for years, each time I read the papers
I'd expect to see his name and once I even
hiked back to find that house again. It was
gone, and with it most of the woods, devoured
by subdivisions spreading from the highway.
But there will always be that last time,
the pile of wings he needed to show me—
his helpless smile and then his shrugging
shoulders as he turned and walked away.

On the Road

*"The only people for me are the... ones who are
mad to live... mad to be saved."* —Jack Kerouac

Someone a lot cooler than I was
gave me a copy my senior year,
probably my friend Jerry, who owned a car
but also read a lot, even subscribed
to magazines like *Atlantic Monthly*.
However it arrived, it was the first book
to keep me up all night, and never again
would I find in print that ache so huge you
could spend your whole life running from it.

Here was a book I wanted to understand—
at the dying end of the 50s in a town
on its way to becoming a suburb,
forever poised next to that larger world
of possibility, but going nowhere.
The only sacred search for kicks I knew
was riding around all night with friends
and 3.2 beer, puffing our Pall Malls,
plotting all the far out things we were
going to do, someday, man, when
we found a way to get it all together.

What we loved best was what we didn't get,
from Zen koans to Marlon in *The Wild One*,
but even in that impossibly male world,
Brando found a girl, the greatest ache
and mystery of them all. Looking back,

perhaps it's not so strange I never got around
to wondering how my father might regard
his own life, commuting to a job he mostly hated.
Or my mother, disappearing even then
into the shadows of her kitchen world.
They'd never heard of Kerouac, didn't go
to movies. There we were, somebody's still life,
each of us waiting for endings we knew
would never come, roads we'd never travel.

Tour Guide

Cartography

Maps have been my storybooks,
from that first time my father spread one
out across the trunk of the car before
some family trip to visit relatives,
which were the only trips we took.
The blue and green stood for lakes and
forests that were seldom on our route,
the open white space, stretches where
I knew I'd keep asking how much longer.
The only mountains in our path were
creases in the paper—no fairgrounds
or ballparks, and none of the names I'd
read about, like New York or Los Angeles.

From the middle of the middle of the
continent, I learned to long for impossible
oceans, the world beyond relations—
never imagining myself here and now,
where that recklessly jagged line on the map
is the one disappearing into the horizon,
inching its miles across the next rise and
the next, ablaze with unbelievable colors,
all the way to the farthest edge.

Hôtel Mercure

Besançon

Why should it be any different
from at home? On the table,
a magazine of poems, abandoned—
every page in first person insistent.
Outside the window, a tree
full of cheeping birds, growing
louder with each rising breeze,
above the TV commentator's news in
indecipherable French. The screen
dissolves to someone's soldiers,
someone's angry crowds with rocks.
Why should it be any different
from at home? Think of all the
ways words fail us—each of us,
fiercely chattering through the night.

Bearings

Ornans

What we notice first is the monument to war dead—
there's one in every town—and then, across the
River Loue, the birthplace of Courbet—pioneer of
realist painting, the tourbook reminds us, political
radical who grew up in a bourgeois house. The small
bridge bears the date 1602—not far away, there are
Roman ruins. It's difficult to get our bearings here.

Yesterday we toured the Museum of the Resistance and
Deportation in Besançon, among a group of silent
soldiers—in the hilltop Citadelle built by the Spanish,
high above the street where Victor Hugo lived. Art
and war, atrocity and sacrifice, strategic and picturesque—
the triple ring of ramparts, the empty watchtowers
where the tourists climb to get a better view.

With the Protestant Reformers

Geneva

Just beyond the giant chess boards in the park
they stare out from a 300-foot stone wall—
Calvin, Knox, even Roger Williams, poised for
each new world. We take the usual photographs
and climb the long hill toward the promenade of
fashionable shops, and then the old district with its
maze of narrowing cobblestone. Beside old cannons
on display is the Hôtel d'Armures and the restaurant
where the U.S. president dined last week—
near the Cathédrale, which holds John Calvin's chair,
the one I walked right by and didn't notice.

On the way back to our garret room I can't help
wonder what the old man would think about
underground parking garages, this world of
precision parts. Tonight I'll dream of chess,
another game I don't play well. I can't make out
my opponent, straight-backed and unyielding
on the other side, yet I know him, all too well.

Excursion Ordinaire

Montreux

Another of those places I've read about,
heard dropped in conversations by those
supposed to know. What they didn't say
was how the *autoroute* takes over everything,
traffic jams the only chance I have to view
the stone-walled vineyards on the slopes,
fairy-tale chateaux, and lowering clouds—
the thought occurs I might as well be home.
Once it was parents who took me places
I didn't think I'd ever go—now it's a rental car,
and roads I can't predict from maps. At Customs,
they simply wave us through without a second look.
In restaurants, I don't know which wine to order,
so I drink the *ordinaire*.

                            At last, the freeway skirts
Chillon, the car is parked, the path leads to a world
of clouds breaking up across the mountain peaks.
A small boat cries its way across the misty lake—
tonight there will be dinner with those I love the most,
and surely, a glass of wine—I can taste it even now—
dry and delicate, amazing my tongue again.

Before the Season

Colmar

It's the second place we've visited they call
the Venice of France—anything with canals,
it seems, quaint houses perched at water's edge.
Too early for the boats, we walk past shops
with postcards showing how it soon will be
or how it must have looked in Medieval times.
Yesterday it was Einsiedeln, the crowds of
pilgrims at the Black Madonna's shrine,
the luck-producing waters we didn't drink.
Back on the road, we drive toward mountains
full of bare trees, no longer certain of the
time or place, no longer caring—the altarpiece
of Issenheim goes with us, a day full of
necessary cloisters. If Venice is the place we
can't imagine, then luck is what we share,
embracing each way as it opens before us.

Our Lady of the Road

Ronchamp

We thought we'd had our fill of churches—
from glowing cherubim to rough-hewn stone,
lurking gargoyles, altars dense with gilded light—
and then, almost an afterthought, we navigated
mountain roads to these massive walls, stark white
in unexpected sun. LeCorbusier's chapel—"a distinct
contrast," the tourbook says, "built to replace
the church destroyed here during World War II."

Ahead, our last kilometers winding through
the Juras, a quiet meal at a familiar *brasserie*—
we've already begun to turn toward home,
the flatlands to the west. Tomorrow is the
day the rental car's due back—we've had
enough of traveling, it's getting late,
and still we walk, our circles lengthening—
for one moment lost, for another found.

Plan de Route

Dijon

Yesterday the students were on strike—
they occupied the *place de ville*, scattering
shoppers with their chants and banners.
Today it's the train—20 kilometers out
and everything is shut down. *Stoppage*,
they call it, and now we ride a bus
on backroads, trying to read the signs.

It's spring here now, weeks ahead of home.
Forsythia blooms along each narrow lane,
fields are plowed, workers move between
the vineyard rows, and every village
bears window boxes full of flowers
close enough to pick as we move by.
At least we're going somewhere,

we tell ourselves—toward traffic snarls,
missed planes and reroutes, tricky headwinds,
more places we didn't think we'd ever go.
Lost among false starts, we watch the
scene beyond the window glass—
scattered clouds, the threat of rain,
and everywhere the bright forsythia.

Fronts

These towns so bright and clean, the picturesque
façades repainted, flower boxes everywhere—
I feel at home though don't know why, perhaps
because my father's family came from here
three generations back—a name, a place, some dates,
though most of it has slipped beyond remembering.

An hour's drive from Munich's flowering parks,
the stark museum at Dachau—I missed it 30 years ago
when traveling some of these same roads with friends.
We stayed at *zimmer frei*—one of which keeps coming back,
near Stuttgart, so strange in its reconstructed newness.
It was run by an old couple, and on their mantel
the single framed photograph of a lost son in uniform.
Eastern Front, the old man shrugged in broken English,
over and over. *You see?* He had no more to say,
and what we needed was to get back on the road—
all those Rhine castles waiting, the Black Forest,
which we wanted to reach while the good light lasted.

Contraries

Bonn
for Sarah

It's hard to believe this broad river
crowded with boats is the Rhine
of legend, but on the drive to Koblenz
the towns are quaint, the hillside castles
picture-perfect—until the stark remains
of the bridge pilings at Remagen,
another monument to war dead.

A contradiction seems to wait
at every turning of the road, even
the thought that long ago some
ancestor looked out on this river,
maybe on his flight from conscription
that would end so many months later
in that dreamland called America.
But what of those who didn't leave—
what war stories would they be telling?

The road winds back to Bonn and
quiet walks from platz to platz
across the cobblestones—or down
to the Rhine to watch the new world
hurrying by on boats and barges.

Old World and New

Amsterdam

One of those places where anything goes,
your friend tells you—from hookers in windows
to pot shops, and on every thoroughfare
restless armies of the young in backpacks.
Just down the street from your hotel you meet
a man so high he flaps his arms and squawks,
tries to take off like one of the herons
cruising for scraps among tethered houseboats.

As nearly empty streets have slowed your pace,
you remember to look where you're going,
the crowds of tall canal houses lined up
to show off their finest clothes—those scenes
you've met before in galleries, as you walk on
and test your clumsy wings, and hold your breath.

History Lessons

Bruges

City of bridges and quaint canals,
one of those places you can't believe
people really live in, inspiring all
the easy metaphors—a movie set,
a postcard or a painting come to life—
but these medieval bricks are no façades
and cobblestones are all too real for tired feet.
Even a tourist café is welcome
respite from November rain and cold—
a serving of the local specialty,
a warming fire, a quiet time to talk.

Not far from here, those Flanders fields
we recited a poem about back in 8th grade—
all the boys from our history class, behind
the curtains of the stage on Veterans' Day.
"We are the dead," we cried in unison,
trying hard to keep from giggling in the dark—
faces that have disappeared across the years,
but not the stern looks of that history teacher,
the only one who knew how lucky we were.

It's growing late and soon enough we'll
settle into train seats, passing close to
Waterloo—only half an hour from our
hotel windows, high above bright umbrellas
making picture postcard patterns in the streets.

Souvenirs

Ghent

Next door to our small hotel
there's a music academy, and
this morning notes from a lone
trumpet drift between the windows
in the narrow street, a melody
so familiar, yet so distant, which
seems to coax the sun from behind
thick clouds for the first time in days.

All along the canal, people sit
with eyes closed and heads tilted
upward, faces bright as the fronts
of buildings behind them. It will be
a day for strolling, stops at small cafés
and crowded shops, a day when
everyone seems a tourist, suddenly
pausing in the middle of the street—

as if to catch these fading notes,
found and lost and found again,
when the first lights flicker on
at dusk, reflected in dark water
and damp cobblestones, across
these many months and miles away.

Work in Progress

Paris

A lovely day for strolling down the Champs
beside a dozen quaint sidewalk cafés
where writers, mostly in berets, are busy
with their notebooks, a glass of wine, pernod—
you can't help feel you've entered more than one
novel, story, poem, perhaps to linger there—
tall man with gray beard, curious, looking like
he has no better place to go. Beyond,
near every monument, the beggars wait—
mostly girls, who hand you soiled pages
speaking of fear for their unborn babies,
the need to get back home, wherever
home might be imagined. All around you
as you walk, words on paper, theirs and yours—
so many different languages and yet
in every one a story that you know.

After a Fall

Glenstal Abbey, County Limerick

Banks of rhododendrons, deepest pink
against a wash of ever-changing green,
and in the mirror pond two swans,
glowing among the mists and shadows.

From the abbey church the voices rise
and fall in unfamiliar cadences,
the Latin vespers with their timeless feel
in shafts of sunlight through an incense haze—
a glimpse of what it must be like
before a fall.
           Just beyond this moment,
boys with rocks are creeping toward those pools,
and even on the quietest country lanes
houses spring up unchecked, with fleets of cars
to join the streaming traffic. So many
here tell stories of the troubled times
that will not go away...
                    but still, there is
the memory of swans and flowers in
perfect light, those voices swelling in song
to celebrate the memory of things
ancient, necessary, forever green.

The Far Shore

Waterville, County Kerry

The massing storm that seemed to follow us
along the narrow mountain roads
has finally broken, not far to the north—
black sky and lightning moving out to sea.

And now the calm of rooms above the beach,
low tide and miles of sand in flat sunlight,
though soon enough, the breakers rumbling in
as other storms sweep by us in the night.

From this far coast the cold Atlantic
stretches out toward home, ever westward,
that unimaginable place so many here
have looked to, beyond all hope of return.

Today, we've come as far as desire and roads
allow. Tomorrow, we'll turn back to plans
and traffic. For now, dreams rise with the tide
and waves breaking at the end of the earth.

Housman's Grave

"And I will friend you, if I may
In the dark and cloudy day."

The roads are narrow through the Shropshire hills,
where Sunday bells have ceased their faithful toll.
Gray skies seem fitting here, deserted towns,
and then the shrine at Ludlow, carved in stone
at St. Laurence's church. Beneath the name
and dates, someone has laid a laurel wreath
atop a garland of spring's briefest white—
for you, who pondered fame and loss so well,
who taught us heart and craft of elegy.
The valley darkens as we drive away
to meet road signs with names we somehow know,
carrying with us the words of a friend—
flowering branches on the shadowed slopes.

Monuments

London

From Covent Garden to Bloomsbury
the names come rolling off the tongue
so familiarly, as if we've known them
all our lives   pilgrims to some lost time,
queuing up among the monuments
with crowds of camcorders and cell phones.

Our cheerful cab driver recites Keats and Blake,
badly, wants to know what we'll remember best—
perhaps the Pizza Hut where that well known
bookstore used to be on Charing Cross Road,
or could it be that charming corner pub
now a part of some international chain?

Or maybe it's what we couldn't tell him—
blossoms on branches just outside the window,
strolls through neighborhoods that missed the guidebooks,
the quiet churches we've had to ourselves,
pondering the stones beneath our feet
where long ago the writing wore away.

Oblate

Whitby Abbey, Yorkshire

Atop these bluffs above the sea, Hilda,
prioress, found this holy place, whose bare
ruined walls still rise beyond two hundred steps
some pilgrims choose to climb up from the town—
from beige to gold in morning light, beside
the lichen-covered gravestones listing back
through centuries along this windy coast,
inscriptions long ago erased by salt.
Caedmon was buried here—poet, brother,
whose name I choose to bear if not his faith.

The stark sun climbs as tour buses snake
their way along the slopes. In the car park,
as we prepare to leave, police have come
to search for teenaged boys with air rifles.
Nothing changes, after all—divine and
human always intertwined. Behind us,
where we didn't walk, Benedictine monks
are gathering for holy offices
no matter what visitors might come and go,
praying even now, for the likes of us.

Mementos

A Box of Photographs

Another group we can't identify—
wistful brides and out-of-focus babies,
an old man with his wagon team, the ones
blank-eyed and stiff in sepia who wait
in studios a hundred years ago.

And then there are the stacks we know by heart—
those old chronologies that show again
the way age marks us all. Faces slacken
as we move along; each mouth strains for smiles—
it's true we're all stunned by the camera now.

Here at last is the one they say was me,
held awkwardly above a birthday cake
by a man in uniform, and then alone
posed in a swing or chair or cap and gown—
confused where he was going even then.

Time to pack the box once more—perhaps we'll
finish sorting it some day and make those
albums for the children—slow progress now,
this pile we throw away, and all the rest
we wonder if we'll recognize again.

Traces

My grandmother used to tell me stories
of her mother's people, the Nortons
from Mayo—who moved to Scotland,
Wisconsin, anywhere. You know the Irish,
she said—too poor to stay at home.

No, I didn't know the Irish,
not even when I went to Dublin,
Galway, Cork—years later, searching
for that trace of recognition
I was so sure would come to me.

You know the Irish, my grandmother said—
we had royalty back there, Lady Jane
Dempsey I think it was, who eloped with
her footman—which doesn't surprise me.
There was a lord, too, though that name's lost.

Everyone from Ireland has royalty somewhere,
she said. And each time I heard them,
those old stories changed again.
I asked my father at her funeral.
She talked to you, not me, he said.

Now *he's* gone, and when my children
ask sometimes, I trace those old tales again,
a little more unsure each journey through.
You know the Irish. It's what we have.
It's all we have. I've come to say it too.

MS Found on a Bottle

Nausea, diarrhea, headache,
or dizziness may occur at first
as your body adjusts
to the medication.

Well, why should I complain?
That's what my grandmother left me—
she who'd always seen a lot worse than
anything I could imagine—and now
as I hold the plastic prescription bottle
I can't help think it should be glass,
substantial, the way Grandma liked things.

If these effects persist
or become bothersome,
inform your doctor.

In all those years I knew her,
every bothersome effect persisted,
especially doctors—never to be trusted
or believed. All she could do was
practice dying on her own—
each new pain the fatal blow,
each visit the last goodbye.

This medication is best taken
with or immediately after meals.

When the time really came
she simply stopped eating,
all she had left to make us believers—
we, the insubstantial ones
who'd never understood prescriptions,
even now, twenty years later,
side effects lingering unchecked.

Pioneer Village

One of those great grandmothers
I never knew was called Betsy—
my wife's name, too—
and in the county plat book
we've finally found her homestead site.
She didn't stay long, heading off
to California nearly 90 years ago.
Now, there's nothing else to mark her
in these acres of antiques,
buildings moved in from all over
the area—schoolhouse, church, and
drygoods store, even someone's jail.
Just another damned museum,
the man in the silly shark hat sighs.
He has to wonder what all this junk
could possibly be worth, his wife
busy photographing everything.
A map, some stories, a set of names—
Great Grandmother, Betsy,
Elverum Township, Pierce County,
North Dakota. Tell me, what's it worth?

Estate Sale

More than 30 plastic bags lined up
beside two hopeless cans—
the garbage men smile politely,
cram three or four in the back of the truck,
then say they'll come back later.

Well, it's their problem now—
ours is all we couldn't bag or give away,
what still fills the house,
just like those places you read about
where the tenants simply vanish,
toast cooling in the toaster,
cigarette burning in an ashtray.

We've worked too many days to find out
what we couldn't save, and tell ourselves again
it's someone else's problem now—
those linens from a long-dead aunt,
a grandmother's costume jewelry,
the diningroom set there's just no place for,
the radio that never worked right—

more than 30 years ago, my father
at the kitchen table sipping his beer
as he listens to the home team on that radio,
his yard gear piled up in the garage,
waiting for the inning
he'll declare it all hopeless
and head outside to work some more.

It's still here—rakes, hoes, shovels,
bags of peat moss, muddy boots.
We'll be far away when the auctioneer
cries it down, all of it—
from never-used wedding gifts
and games nobody's played for years,
to closets full of clothes that just don't fit.

It's such a big yard, someone says,
as everything shrinks in the rearview mirror—
the moment we remember
we won't be coming back.

Another Zoo Story

The children couldn't stand the smell,
while their mother preferred to watch people.
Who could blame her—that blue-veined,
brash, and bulging crowd, eating
their way and strewing a trail,
all laughs and shouts from cage to cage,
as if they were changing channels.
Once it was different, I tried to believe—
looking back to the chalky outline
of my own childhood. There I stood,
so hopelessly green, stunned
to see the monkeys do so casually
what I'd only heard about on streetcorners.
Even then, when I really think about it,
most of the animals were mangy, asleep,
or crazy-eyed in their endless pacing.
Isn't it amazing what we need to forget
so that someday we can repeat it?
Tell me again, if we're having such fun,
then why must we feel like weeping?

Engines

Sometimes my father took me to see them—
those big new diesels, downtown at the
Milwaukee Road station, where sleek
passenger trains would always thrill me too,
people boarding in such handsome clothes,
looking so happy and important, heading off
somewhere I couldn't imagine going.

Then we'd stop to watch the steam engines,
my father and I—all their busy chuffing
around the yards. But I already knew
steam engines, from the tracks not far from home,
where my friends and I would stand on the bridge
to wait for them, losing ourselves in steam and smoke.

I never told my father of those days above the tracks
when everything would disappear, how we'd shout
and dance for those delirious moments. And now,
when the haze finally clears, it's gone—all of it,
even that huge old station standing derelict downtown,
as if I too have boarded one of those fast trains—
heading to a place where no one knows me,
all timetables coming apart in my hands.

Inheritance

My mother poses in her riding boots
sixty years ago beside a small Montana shack.
Just beyond the photograph I know
are horses and a dog half-coyote,
jugs of homemade wine, and rattlesnakes—
whose severed tails provided years of
show-and-tell for children bred in cities.
That was before you even were a thought,
my father used to tease, but how I loved
that picture anyway—from the first time
I imagined a life beyond the one we all wore
every day.
        Fifty years or more my mother
stored her boots in a basement box—
memento of what was, what might have been
before the war changed everything. I keep
those rattles now, for both of us,
still take them out from time to time,
forever strange and thrilling to the touch.

Any Day Now

Like so many of their generation,
my parents learned to live by what they had
to give up. Long after they could afford it,
they still couldn't bring themselves to buy
something not on sale. My father tore his
paper napkins in two and saved half for
another meal. My mother was an expert
on every off-brand on the grocery shelves.
And all those retirement trips they never took,
right up until the cancer robbed my father
of everything, his voice fading into
phone static, still promising that visit,
the one they were going to make any day now.

Lately, I hear that voice more and more often.
And there's the dream that sometimes comes with it,
the one where my father and I are driving
somewhere for a visit in his old black Ford,
a place I probably don't want to go,
and we never speak a word between us,
even when something amazing passes
the windows. But it's all right, because there's
still a chance we'll say something important
to each other. How I wish we understood that,
both of us back then, saving our pennies
and somehow squandering all the rest.

Memory Care Unit

"I don't know where I'm supposed to be,"
she says, beginning her rosary of
wringing hands. If past is prologue,
then tomorrow is the day that never comes.

Myrtle simply babbles, fiercely
carpet sweeping clean wood floors
while Alma's off again to find
the sister she knows is waiting
somewhere just behind closed doors.
Jean's the cheerful one, proud to
remember piano tunes across the years
but not the face she talked to last.
"Where are you from?" she asks and
then replies "that's good" to every answer.

Enter here a world of women alone so long
they gather round each visitor, transfixed
by the flicker of something almost familiar,
as if whispers alone can hold them up.

"Where am I supposed to be?" she asks,
trusting me for any answer. I take her hand
and we recite those necessary names again:
mother, *son*, *right here*, *right now*, and *always*.

Incoming

For weeks, predictions change each day—
who *really* knows how high the river's going to
rise this time? Everyone has a theory—
wet fall, early spring, the threat of ice jams
and new storms moving in. All over town,
the cries of bulldozers pushing up dikes,
crews of sandbaggers hurrying by in trucks.
Every station on every dial sends out
the call for pumps and volunteers.

Today, the national guard troops fan out
through neighborhoods with evacuation alerts.
Basement floor cracks ooze the water
rising from beneath us. Up river,
more rumors and reports are massing.
It's all we know, all we talk about,
filing from our houses, transfixed by
darkening skies, the fierce black choppers
bursting just above the tossing treetops.

The Tribe

Beyond the hedge, from early this morning,
small boys in another yard are whooping
and banging on something—from stone
to wood to metal, they thwack incessantly.

I try to remember when it was like that—
the day, perhaps, my friends and I
threw our best marbles against a brick wall,
one by one, hoping they wouldn't break,

but each time heaving them harder.
Beyond the dark tangle of leaves,
children's voices rise again above
the steady beating, and somewhere

a mother is calling—theirs, mine—
calling to all of us who should
know better but somehow don't,
who should know when it's time

to come in, to go out, to be quiet.
And now, at last, we're driven indoors—
heads down, heels dragging, amazed
at all this silence, guilty as charged again.

Lost and Found

"Some keep the Sabbath going to Church—
I keep it staying at home—"
                    —Emily Dickinson

Sunday morning, blues on the radio—
I know that tune too well,
buried in my chair with football scores
while all the family sleeps.
What's lost is found and lost again,
the Sunday morning paradox—
between the then and now,
the stop and start again,
a church bell and a mouth harp toll.

I sit with news I didn't want to read—
threats of war and promises no one will keep.
Furnace surges, snowflakes gather
on the window sill, a jet plane rattles glass,
and all the house is fast asleep.

Constellations

I have forgotten how early darkness comes
these first days of December. On my walk
home from work at five o'clock, fresh snow
lies unshoveled under the streetlights,
covered with small tracks in all directions.
Every window I pass is streaked with light
from a TV screen, every single window.

Under the porch light of my own house
there are more tracks, dozens of tracks
on the steps, right up to the front door.
How much more have I managed to forget?
The snowflakes drop straight down now,
gathering together as they fall.

Winter Count

for Jay and Martha

Each summer I keep the bird book close,
though pictures rarely look like what I see—
colors not quite right and variations
much too similar to choose from. These past
few winters I've hung a feeder near the
kitchen window and watched pine siskins
every day, those birds I knew would come.

This year the snow's too deep for me to reach it—
the feeder hangs empty, swings in wind,
the only thing I'm certain will return, while
leafless hedges fill with sparrows celebrating sun—
like train whistles, those steady choruses
I don't usually hear. It takes a visitor to tell me
what a noisy place I choose to live in,
or to notice that snow shovel in the garage,
the one half-eaten from years of scraping walks.

Sparrows, shovels, and the cries of trains—
what's always there but seldom seen,
and now, these words so tentative across
the stark notebook pages, retrieved
from where I left them months ago.
Before spring thaw I'll send them out—
to friends who live beside a frozen lake,
whose own bird book lies well-thumbed
on a sunny table, who also know in seasons
cold beyond belief how the most familiar
sounds and movement call us back so suddenly
from places we've forgotten having been,
to clear at last each drifted-over path.

The Wall between Us

"He moves in darkness as it seems to me."
—Robert Frost

Late in the afternoon of Halloween
my new neighbor stops by to introduce
himself at the front door. At first I think
it must be an early trick-or-treater—
a young father with his small son in tow,
both staring at our grinning jack o'lantern
and then the bowl of brightly-wrapped candy.
Take some, I say, but the father says no,
sharply—they have their own candy at home,
and besides, they don't participate in
godless rituals. He's simply here to
give me notice he's putting up a fence
between our two backyards—mostly for dogs,
he says, two Labradors who'll need the space.
But not to worry about any noise—
they'll be fitted with special collars
which will shock them if they dare to bark.
When I joke about the line *good fences
make good neighbors*, he simply stares, then says
the Lord has blessed him with a growing family.

True to his word, a six-foot high board fence
goes up in days, followed by the dogs,
so strangely silent in their circling
and endlessly alone—I can't help feeling
glad weeks later when I hear that one of them
escaped, and gladder still to find out that
my neighbor bought the house to fix it up

for quick resale. He'll be gone by spring—
but for his pamphlets on finding the Lord,
a fence that casts long shadows in the yards,
and a small boy's eyes, darting hopelessly
from a bowl of candy to his father's frown.

Labor Day

It sounds like it's raining in the woods
long after the heavy clouds have passed,
the drops cascading noisily through leaves
all morning, and the leaves falling too,
already maple red and aspen gold
this Labor Day. Too soon, too soon,
the lake birds seem to call—the loons
that need a quarter-mile of wing-slapping,
wing-rowing takeoff to get themselves
airborne. Everything here seems so firmly
in gravity's grip, and now the rain
again, for real this time—I can almost
hear the wail of children all around me
that their last good weekend's ruined.
School starts tomorrow, the day I hated
most, the requiem for all that imaginary
summer freedom. But I didn't have much
to carry with me in those days, had yet
to feel the true weight of things, or even
know the blessing of a gentle rain in
a dry season, no matter when it comes—
here, alone, on this screened-in porch thrust out
toward the drop-rippled lake, thinking only
a moment about tomorrow and all
those other things that weigh me down, that soon,
too soon, I'll have to start giving away.

Finding My Way

Because I can't sleep in hotel rooms
I've come to use ear plugs and pills,
and sometimes when I wake
at 4 in the morning, I'm startled
by the waves of my own blood
breaking on the shores of my eardrums.

Today there's that sound again,
only I'm home, in my own bed
and it's long past sunrise. It has
to be snow, a lot of snow in the night
muffling the waves of traffic
on the busy street at the corner.

Can you blame me if I don't get up
and look? How rare it is to be
certain of exactly where you are,
to fall back asleep free of panic,
and dream, perhaps, of a lake
in August, curtains flapping
from an open window, and beyond,
the pulse of wind in leaves and water.

True Colors

Near Marvin, South Dakota, 3-11-02

The prairie sky has turned to heavy gray,
sagging into frozen lakes and matted brown.
Today the world is icy, dull, and even
the familiar trees and farms and towers
seem far away. No birdsong, no train cry,
and for the moment nothing moves except
a black pickup truck with bedsheet-sized flag
streaming behind it—the red of wounds,
the white of snow across the tops of hills,
the blue of better days. It says again
that times have changed forever, even here,
where church bells startle silence, and fish,
like the oldest promises we know, are
circling under ice—silver, gold and green.

Keeping Track

*"Your way of life should be different
from the world's way."*
                                    —St. Benedict

for Brother Gene

Seven days of heat have broken,
the paper says, working statisticians
overtime. But there are no records
this morning, save those on radios
along the puddled streets—a few cars
hurrying home to throbbing bass notes.
Barely awake, I've walked out among
air-conditioner drones to meet the sunlight
cresting treetops, and a pair of neighbors
who look up from front-porch coffee
and wave, shyly—all of us startled
to share what we thought was ours alone.
Soon enough, the world will turn its
workday self to things more urgent
than yards with heavy-headed peonies
and bird songs never heard before,
these few words I've finally found
to fill the blank space on my calendar:
summer's second day, the one whose
cool, sweet dawning drew me like a prayer.

Long Distance

for Katie

Near midnight, our daughter calls
to say she's safely home again—
600 miles of interstate, with storms
so bad at times that she could barely
follow the tail-lights in front of her.
She wishes she'd had that moon
to guide her—the one we watched
two nights ago in its full, bright rising.
Later, she even walked out to find it again,
and then, inevitably, we reminded her
about another night—that first moon-walk,
when she was only a baby and her mother
held her in front of the TV on her lap
so one day she could say she saw it too—
something truly amazing. Then, as now,
beyond the window and the glowing screen,
that bright face in the sky, better than a star
to wish on—for daughters, miles, and years,
and whatever else we can only begin to imagine.

Mark Vinz was born in Rugby, North Dakota, grew up in Minneapolis and the Kansas City area, attended the Universities of Kansas and New Mexico, and since 1968 has taught at Minnesota State University Moorhead, where he also served as the first coordinator of the university's Master of Fine Arts in Creative Writing program.

His poems, stories, and essays have appeared in numerous magazines and anthologies, and he is the author of six chapbook collections of poems as well as the full length collections *Climbing the Stairs*, *Mixed Blessings*, *Late Night Calls* (prose poems), *Minnesota Gothic*, and *Affinities* (the last two in collaboration with photographer Wayne Gudmundson). He edited the poetry journal *Dacotah Territory* during the 70s and since then has been editor for Dacotah Territory Press, which has published a number of short collections by writers in the region. He is also the co-editor of several anthologies, including *Common Ground: A Gathering of Poems on Rural Life*; *Beyond Borders: New Writing from Manitoba, Minnesota, Saskatchewan, and the Dakotas*; *Inheriting the Land: Contemporary Voices from the Midwest*; *Imagining Home: Writing from the Midwest*; *The Party Train: An Anthology of North American Prose Poetry*; and *The Talking of Hands: Unpublished Writing by New Rivers Press Authors*.

A recipient of a National Endowment for the Arts fellowship in poetry, he has also won the New Rivers Press Minnesota Voices competition, Milkweed Editions' "Seeing Double" competition, six Pen Syndicated Fiction awards, and three Minnesota Book Awards. In the spring of 2005, Larry Woiwode named him an Associate Poet Laureate of North Dakota.